Dreams for Sale

November 2009

Dear Linda,

after all these years. So grad to reconnect and to know how wonderful your life is.

May life's blessings continue to ~~shower~~ SHOWER you and all you love!

xo

JoAnne

Pg. 79

Dreams for Sale

Poems and Lyrics

Jo Anne Kurman

Editor: Nancy Carleton, nancycarleton.com
Cover Art and Illustrations: Chris Davies
Cover Design: Dave Blake, Berkeley, Calif.
Cover Photograph: Ute, Face Studios Photography
Book Design & Composition: Dave Blake, Berkeley, Calif.
Print Management: Dave Blake, Berkeley, Calif.

To order additional copies of *Dreams for Sale*,
visit amazon.com; to place a wholesale order,
contact BookSurge at 866-308-6235.

Library of Congress Control Number: 2009903172
ISBN 1-4392-3573-2

Printed in the United States of America.
10 9 8 7 6 5 4 3 2 1

Contents

LYRICS

To the loving memory of my beloved friend
Milly St. Charles
1919–2009

For my part I know nothing with any certainty,
but the sight of the stars makes me dream.

Vincent van Gogh

Preface

A significant part of my life has been devoted to writing poems and lyrics. As a singer/songwriter, I've had the opportunity to perform songs I've written, and so, when I write lyrics, it's always with the awareness that they will be heard in public. Writing poetry has been a more private and personal form of expression, and so I've kept most of my poems tucked away in bedroom drawers.

For most of my life, I've dreamed that one day my book of poetry would be published, but the idea of combining my poems and lyrics in the same book was a recent and an exciting epiphany. My dream got bigger by allowing it to be more than what I originally conceived it would be. I believe there's a right time for everything, and more often these days I'm paying closer attention to those divine nudges.

Poetry and lyrics are closely married yet unique at the same time. Writing a lyric and putting it together with music is an intricate craft. Once in a while a song seems to write itself, but usually it takes me weeks or sometimes months to complete. The challenge is telling a full story in a lyric when the song will last just a few minutes.

Poetry is an "anything goes" art form, and I love the freedom that comes with no rules. Without music leading the words, or words leading the music, there's a wild abandon in expressing uncensored feelings, which at times has been a deeply cathartic experience for me. Unlike the long, agonizing process that can be involved in completing a song, I usually write my poems in one sitting, with a free-flowing style of consciousness. It might be said that poetry is the lyric of the writer's heart, with each reader bringing to it his or her own melody.

And so I offer my book of poems and lyrics to you now.

They touch on loss, hurt, wonder, love, passion, and God—
a tapestry of my life tied up in a bow, which I bring to you
with an open heart.

Jo Anne Kurman
Summer 2009

Acknowledgments

It is only in writing my first book and experiencing the unique partnership with an editor firsthand that I can now add to the chorus of writers who have gone before me in expressing their deepest gratitude. Without the brilliant guidance of my editor, Nancy Carleton, this book would have been just a homegrown pamphlet. Nice, but not the book you are holding in your hands, which I so proudly present.

To Chris Davies, my heartfelt gratitude for blessing my book with your gorgeous illustrations.

To Dave Blake, for making my book look like a dream-come-true. To Donna Strong, my "gate." To Rick Streitfeld, for being my advocate all those years ago. To Barbara Borax, the wind beneath my wings. To Bert Danon, for always believing. To Don Raymond, for pointing the way. To Lori Donato, my soul sister and fellow student of life. To Paul Nielsen, for your generosity of spirit and eagle eye. To Mike Meyer, the eleventh-hour man. To Carmen Renee Berry and Jordan Paul, for taking the time to review the final draft of my manuscript and for your support of my work.

To these amazing individuals whose love and support inspired me to complete this book: Kay Finer, Carol Shaw, Adrianne Mitchell, Melissa Johnson, Chris Cooper, Corliss Lee — and to all those persons with whom I continue to share my life's journey.

Thank you, all!

Jo Anne Kurman

POEMS

Chance Meetings

Dreams for Sale

The vast wasteland of dreams.

Burnt-out, tired dreams,
They laid down their colors,
Put them in storage,
For happier souls to wear.

Singing in a Bar

He sat and stared at me.
People always looking at me—
How comical when you see it
Through misty, tired, sung-out eyes.
Funny, it makes me cry:
What goes on in their minds—
The men who stare?
Fantasy, lust, respect?
Or are they only remembering?
Oh well,
My job is to be the singer.

And their job is to stare.

San Francisco

Hills with roller-coaster streets
That dead-end into the wharf.
Bed and breakfast,
No phones, and *Annie*.

A still silhouette of cigarette smoke.
A black cat and I in a locked gaze.

Hello, San Francisco,
I've returned once again.
I've come to ride your trolley cars
And be with my friends,
Who walk on you every day.

The Old Man

The old man stares through the window.
Clutching at a curtain,
He looks at the world
And feels the nurse's hands.

Staring, he doesn't blink,
Just stands in his nightshirt,
So still, in his little pink
Stucco house with overgrown lawn.

A ball rolls in his yard.
A boy runs and picks it up.
For a moment they see each other;
The boy laughs and runs away.

The old man remembers—
For a moment he recalls.
A tear rolls down his cheek.
His eyes follow
Until he sees nothing at all.

Distant Cities

Back on track,
A new train is coming.
She whistles loud
As she passes all the lies,
As she whirls past pointed fingers of blame,
And the shame
That built dark clouds
On distant cities now,
Never to remain,
Nestled deep in her heart,
Where coals glow hot
With a fire of Self—
The eternal flame.

Lace Curtains

She stirs behind lace curtains,
Once tied up neatly with velvet bows—
A delicately patterned woman,
Fallen behind draperies of time.

A sliver of light at the opening,
A shadow of a girl she once knew,
Frightened by fate yet denying
Limbs going slower, ever slow.

She keeps watch at the window
As life slips by day by day,
Afraid of what may defile her,
Yet longing for a simple hello.

She catches her face in the mirror
And gathers her strength at the door.
She trembles as she takes her steps
Into the sunlight,
Along her pathway,
Beyond lace curtains,
Straight down the sidewalk of life.

Jakarta

Jakarta in the springtime—
Where rain and heat meet to make steam and sweat,
Where pollution is a devil with tired hands,
Black with filth and grime.

Hot, I unbutton my blouse.
My clothes have become one with my skin.
The heaviness of the air hangs everywhere,
Sitting on me.

I get up to make tea,
But someone unseen
Leads me back to my chair:
"Be still now and listen; this is only a dream."

I feel my body.
The wet air makes me aware of my weight,
Every inch I must take, every inch I create.
Every day I move slowly in a place time hates.

The jungle drums beat out my thoughts.
How long have I been here?
Forever I will stay
With the people of yesterday.

My Indonesian brothers smile and say,
"No problem, man, this is the forgotten land.
We will return to from whence we came —
No one to blame, no one to blame."

I will get up and walk away,
But my soul remains, caught in between.
Caught in my throat, the words cannot come:
I am your mother, you are my son:
Jakarta, look what the white man has done.

Ashamed, I bow my head and cry.
Too late for tears, your plight is mine.
Let me hold you for now
And tomorrow — tomorrow
We will fix the broken bow.

A Blonde American in Indonesia

There are too many people here—
A purity of race looking as one.
I am a stranger amongst these
Endless faces in this human sea.

Masses of flesh,
Of fingers and feet.
They want to touch me.
They want to meet me.
They want to be me.

The look of want unmasked
In their eyes
Wide open in their simple request:
Please take me with you to your country.
We want to go
Now,
For we, too,
Want the best.

A Hole in the City

There's a hole in the city
That no one sees,
Where no one goes.
Nothing lives there;
Nothing grows.

It's getting bigger every day,
And people just turn their heads away.

It's not pretty—
This hole in the city:
The darkness and the void
Every time a hungry baby dies,
A street person cries,
Every time a drug goes into a vein
And being kind is called insane.

It gets a little wider—
The hole in the city.
It gets a little deeper—
The hole in the city.
The hole in the city
That no one sees,
Where no one goes.

Lady of Dreams

Can you speak now?
Can you explain why you sit there,
Folded hands,
Head on your chest,
Eyes closed?
Has life been too long,
Lady of Dreams?

Has life disappointed?
Are you tired and worn-out?
Can you rally one more time?
One more time can you get up
And walk straight into your heart?

See her now:
She lifts a finger
So slightly it rises up
And then settles back down
Into her hands folded
Into the silence.

The Way to Go Is Free

The lost city in someone's lost dreams
Is calling to me from the Land of Opportunity,
The Land of No Regret, with no tomorrow;
Sound your trumpets loud.

The prophets sing their songs on high—
How majestic and how proud.
They speak in all tongues
And tell us the time is nigh
Not to tarry here long on empty lots—
The wasteland from coast to coast,
Dry and parched with no sky.
Time to bring home the pretty words.

They falsely ring in our ears;
They sound so sad and absurd.
Sing out the sound of the soul.
Shout it out and make it clear.

The way to go is free.
The way to go is free.
Joining the church of humanity,
The way to go is free.

The apple trees have lost their roots;
They softly cry and heave and sigh.
They have no soil, they have no ground—
Nowhere to lay their sorrow down.

The American dream has drifted away
On ships of fools to other shores,
Where light and laughter disappear
And night is king of sun and day.

Is this what we have when life is done:
To win the "race of faster" at last,
With no taste, no touch, no sight—
With no chance to do it again?

The prophets are silent now.
We cannot pretend to heed their warnings
While continuing to devour all life
At the Feast of Killing the Morrow
For the sake of now.

The way to go is free.
The way to go is free.
Joining the church of humanity,
The way to go is free.

An Old Kindred Soul

One fearless knight,
One romantic fool.
Two clowns in a circus—
The vagabond rules.

Run in the wind.
Stop when you see
A gypsy reclining
On life's endless leaves.

I pause to take rest
With an old kindred soul—
To freshen my spirit
With one whom I've known.

Be strong, noble knight.
This lady bows low
In humble appreciation
To an old kindred soul.

The Bar Singer

Two days past Christmas,
One hour past midnight,
The last song is sung.

Three people at the bar:
Quietly, a girl laughs in the corner
As a quarter slides into the jukebox.

Chance Meeting

Encounter with a female club singer talking to a handsome male customer. Sparks are flying.

"Hello, it's nice to meet you. Are you from England? Compact discs? Huh. You must be very high tech. Thank you for listening. I'll sing those Dylan and Baez songs for you."

Inner dialogue of same female club singer talking to same handsome male customer. Sparks are flying.

"Hello, I'd love to kiss your mouth and feel your lips on mine. What will we do when we touch? Will we know a familiar softness? Will I shudder when we are eye to eye? I want to know your English-speaking tongue on mine."

As she desires him, he watches her walk away.

Rainbows of Love

Rainbows of Love

I want to give to you.
I'm awaiting your arrival
With not a lot of calmness.

I feel you hear me but cannot see you,
Spirit preceding form.

The anticipation is great—
It makes my heart swell with
Desire and longing.

I send you rainbows of love
Waking and sleeping.
I play you a song only you can
Hear, only meant for your ears.

Come to me now, my lifemate
Of my life.
I am ready and have been in
Preparation.
Now.
Come now.
Now come.
Now.

Man

I still await your company.
When will you appear?
Come near
And speak my name.
I will know
When I hear your voice.
Say it now.
I will love you deeply
Forever and today.

Falling

Fortune smiled
And there you stood,
So close and the stirring
Of something good filling the air,
Distant sounds of love
Flickering softly in your eyes.

A promise unspoken in your hands
As you outlined the air,
Of hopeful times to come.

We watched each other.
The signs were small,
Yet yearning grew.
It filled the room
With silent hearts aching
From rumors of yesterday—
Both afraid.
Then you reached out.
We touched.
The rites of
Falling,
Falling,
Falling in love.

Your Arms

I knew the wind then;
It was at my back.
My steps were light;
I knew the way.
The path was clear,
My thoughts were light,
The road was straight,
And I flew
Into your arms.

Letting In

How long I have waited for this moment,
And the moment is here.
The anticipation of the next move
Makes my heart beat faster.
The pounding resounds in my soul,
Quickening my step.
Shadows at my shoulders,
Wishing them away,
Doubts brushing my face,
The angels sigh and say:
Let love in, let love in.
The old way to wrestle and die,
Carving new patterns in virgin soil,
Your laughter leading the way.

Two Roses

Blooming together in time,
Our hearts on the same line of rhyme
Became complete when one met the other—
Not to keep, not to have,
But to mirror the brother,
To mirror the sister
And friend and lover.

How splendid to watch you,
To witness your opening,
The rain washing out sorrow forgotten.
Now be gone, now forever.
Pain has become the joy,
And joy is the measure
Our hearts now treasure.

So, my beloved soulmate in time,
I welcome you here, for always be mine.
I will learn to love you without capturing.
I love you, be free.
I love you, for seeing me.
I simply and truly love you.
Love you.

Who Lives Alone

You have a way about you.
You have a way that turns me around
To something
I've never known could touch me.

Me, the one who fights alone,
Who says that heartaches are for those
Who haven't learned.

Well, I have a joke for you—
The kind that isn't funny.
I thought I knew,
But now I know
I'm just among the many fools
Who live alone.

You have a way of touching.
You have a way that tells me
I'm the lucky one
Who never thought of something—

Something, we were never taught,
That says living is for those who give
And may get nothing.

Who knows what we may do
When love surprises us?
What will I do when he appears?

I thought I knew, but now I'm afraid.
I may be in the parade of fools.
Oh please, don't let me be another,
Just another lonely number
Of one
Who lives alone.

Moments

I wait.
The time is in moments,
Not minutes,
Not hours and days.

Oh, this time we spend away
From each other is so hard.
To see why we must be like this—
I know it best.

Because love grows while apart
And will continue
Until our eyes meet each morning
And our breath mingles into oneness.

Knowing the closeness of you,
Each moment forever in your arms
I love
The breathtaking oneness
Of us.

Soul Song

Filling my spirit with
The circle energy,
Connecting the searching call
Of yang,
Complete and full;
Of light,
Brilliantly bright—
Welcome answer to my soul song.
I bow in humble acceptance
To my completeness.

You and Me

A memory was made,
A promise was kept,
That you would be there,
And the heart said yes.

Yes, to the coming.
Yes, to the moving out.
No fear, no asking,
Only pure and so true.

I will never forget—
You asked that I not;
We will always be
A part of heaven.

You
And me.

Mine

A flower bloomed today;
I don't know its name.
I never saw it until now,
But I think I'm going to
Love it more
Than anything before.

It will never leave me—
My flower.
My heart complete,
My true love,
My own,
Mine.

Now that You Are Here

I've looked for you—
The shadow of a man I used to know,
Streaked within the sunsets of days going by,
Caught in the faces of strangers
And in the laughter of friends.

Never dreaming until I dreamed
You were there with me,
Where lost lovers live,
Within the arms of freedom,
Where hearts know no boundaries.

It has always been;
I have never left.
Love has welcomed me home
To at last have what is mine returned.
All is well now, my soul.
I can rest
Now that you are here.

I Will Be Home

A cold note.
Santa Monica skies,
Flat land, white stars,
Clear and twinkling.
Again I am thinking
Beyond the clouds,
Beyond time and tears
And back to when
All is joy,
All is love.
That time is not here.
He is gone,
But I will,
I will always be,
I will be home.

Arrows

The heart it knows;
It swells with pride
And falls when pierced
With arrows of wicked love,
Wrenched clear from fresh
Sorrow.

How quick one goes from
High love,
So young and new,
To the deep tunnels of
Regret.

Escapees

Where do people go who have loved?
Where do they gather after they care?
Where is that place, that somewhere
Deep in the sea of souls forgotten?

Maybe loving someone is just an escape
From the awful aloneness.

No wonder we lose our minds to love.

Unlove

It races through her soul like leprosy,
Eating away bit by bit all sense of decency,
All form of good and righteousness.
Oh, the temple of flesh
Succumbs to the wateriness of heavy sighs,
Of the darkened thighs
Of mystery.

To be rid of the force unseen in her breasts
Would be a day of freedom, indeed—
Free to be with men without wanting to
Taste them, caress them, and beat them
With her raw, burning lust.

For just one moment of peace,
What must she do to be free?

Free to know she is enough,
Free to be a part of humanity,
Free to see souls and not bodies,
Free to love herself—
Free, free of the empty wasteland,
Of the wicked,
The loneliness,
The Godforsaken land
Of Unlove.

I Knew Love Once

I knew love once.
I knew the sound;
It called to me.
I ran so hard I couldn't breathe.
It knew my name
And touched my hair—
Said it would follow me anywhere.

So off we went
Down the road of dreams;
Galloping on clouds,
Our clear eyes gleamed.
No thought for the morrow,
We reveled in the day.
How sweet youth is—
How sweet and gay.

I knew love once.
It tickled my chin
And grabbed me hard—
Said we'd always win.

I knew love once.
Yes, I knew love once.

Then and Now

Then
It was always,
And the nights, like promises unspoken
Each one—
The anticipation not greater
Than the hot kisses and embraces we shared.
Love was there.

The quiet walk in a world so white
That we stole from time,
And through our eyes now we can conjure up
Like sorcerers
When we remember—
Remember
We were young
And life was new
And, oh, how I loved you.

Now
I look into the dewdrops on the petals
Of three roses,
And I see the beauty of what still is—
The years apart,
The pain and the sorrow.

The look of surprise when we speak of tomorrow:
Yesterday is gone;
Today is where we stand.
And now I'm a woman,
And you are a man.

At This Passing

I'll never see you again
But on a new day in another land;
When the hills are green on the horizon,
You will be running to me,
The gift of love in your hands.

Closer, closer, I've yet to see your face,
But I know it is you.
I don't need to see, just feel.
Our music rings together
Beyond time and forever.

You taught me to express with my hands
The delicacy of a finer tune yet played.
Oh, my friend, you believed when I didn't;
Your knowing helped me know me—
Undying, your faith and love.

Not this time around, my true man,
Not this time for embrace
But to teach me my lessons
Through guitar strings—
A more subtle expression,
The melodic nuances
Of love.

Merging

Be one with me.
You, and you
And that, and that.
My arms are reaching
All around me at once,
And the air feels
Thin and empty.
What will fill them if not
You?
What will last?
What will grow forever?
Who will care always?
We change, we move,
We need to grow.
Discovering detachment,
I am walking on new ground.
What a fragile, yet incredibly
Powerful thing faith is,
Born in the love of God.

Day and Night

Day and Night

There are no more stars in the sky,
But that doesn't mean that they don't shine.
The sun just took them all for a ride
On his sunny rays of bright time.

The moon danced in her silver slippers,
And the golden dipper sang a tune.
They all jumped and rocked together,
And decided to come back and do it again real soon.

And they called it day
'Cause it rhymed with play.

Then the sun got tired and closed his eyes
And told the stars, "Rise again in the sky."
And as they did, they sang him a lullaby,
And the moon watched with a mother's pride.

Together they make the darkness bright —
A very special thing to do —
The stars and mother moon
To light the way for me and you.

And they called it night
'Cause it sounded right.

So when you're feeling alone and want to cry,
Remember our friends way up high in the sky.
They're singin' and dancin' and lighting our way
And calling to us, "Won't you come out and play?"

"We love you, don't be blue," you can hear them say.
"We love you forever, 'cause we're made that way.
Come dance in the moonlight, come dance in the sun;
We shine for you all because life was made for fun."

Sleepy Owl

Sleep will not take me.
It waits patiently in the corner.
Only when it is ready
Will it creep up to my
Lying body and spread
Its fingers over my eyes.

It lets me go free.
It takes me to dreams
Yet undreamed.
It is the messenger
Of sweet nothingness.

To the Light

I feel mad.
I feel the madness.
It is everywhere—
On each wooden stair
Leading up to the attic
Of darkness and despair.

Quietly close the door
And softly steal back;
Down the flight,
Even with the fright.
Keep walking,
Keep walking,
Keep walking back down
To the light.

The Plagiarist

I have been stolen from by one
Who laughs and twirls about
And says thank-yous to young girls
Who gush and wish they could be her.

But she is a thief with two faces of Eve:
Her mask is long and wide;
The real self she is sure to hide—

A masquerade of deceit.

Don't turn your head;
She'll be there to grasp
Whatever true that your hand makes,
And she'll call it her own.
But deep in her bones,
The cancer will grow—
The cancer of a lost,
Blackened soul.

Temptation

Doubts fill my mind,
Flying like bats,
Hitting my eyes,
Blinding my perception of
Right and wrong.

Unruly thoughts,
Tossing me about
Into the deep darkness of night,
Poisoning my goodness,
Making me want what is evil.

Evil veiled in changing forms,
Making precious the desires
Of little men—
The ones who fill their chests
With empty treasures,
Moaning for riches that could have been
If only they'd lied to their neighbors
Or cheated their friends.
The loss of their souls too small a price to pay?

God bless the humble man and woman,
For they are the rulers of the universe in infinite spirit.
Forever may they reign.

Give It Away

She will let it shine forever now—
The love she feels for humanity.

It pours over cities,
Babies, and turtles—
All the little things unseen
And all the great cathedrals.

And back into her heart and around
Her sorrows, till bubbles of laughter
Come floating up and out, sailing
High over the broken people,
And then bursting in a downpour
Of giggle rain falling on
The sad and lonely,
Wondering why their hearts feel lighter.

And one day a smile lit up the sky
From one who got caught in the storm
And forgot her umbrella.

To Be Me

I am cynical,
A bit hostile,
Very negative:
Is this me?

This crossroads of being
Has made me more conscious,
And I'm caught in between.

Not wanting to be them
But desperately needing them,
I fool myself
With conversations of wit
While the storm inside rages
And then it subsides.

I yearn
To explode in beauty
With creativity spewing out
Like hot lava,
Molten and alive in me—
The black and the white
And the gray
Of me.

Echoes

Oh, blackness,
Where did you go?
Now that the light
Has cast out your eerie
Darkness?

Oh, fear,
Did you think you made
Your home permanent
In my soul?

I can't hear you now.
Your voice has weakened
In the rays of deep
Laughter—
The healing sounds of
Love made while
Feeling life all around.

Light of Hope

The light shines patiently
On the porch of desire.
It quietly waits in the night
For a friend—
A shadow,
A moth who touches lightly,
Teasing with silky wings.

Dark Side of the Moon

On the dark side of the moon
Is a bird that flies low—
The one that you see,
The one that you know.

Careful not to pretend
He's not what he is;
He knows he's a bird
That flies low.

But he dreams of the light
And the height up above,
Where he's free to fly as high
As he dares to go.

But when he awakens,
The stillness and the black
Are there to remind him
Of visions he lacks.

If he never awakened,
The real world would be there,
And here would become
The unreality bare.

On the dark side of the moon
Is a bird that flies low—
The one that you see,
The one you don't know.

Fields of Daisies

I will lay me down
To slumber in fields of daisies
Ne'er to wake up, no more.
A hush so still—
No hurt, just sun;
No pain, just light;
No sad, just daisies,
Bending and blowing in the wind.

I will lay me down
To slumber in fields of daisies
And dream of better days.

Wings of Midnight

My beautiful bird has flown away.
I lift my hands up to help him in his flight.
Standing here watching until he's out of sight,
Listening for his wings of return—
Wings of midnight.

Old Owls

A whistler in the night
Round about three:
Who can hear it
But old owls like me?

Stars, Stars, Stars

They wait for no one,
Nor do they wait
For anything to happen.
Patiently, they hang
Suspended in time
Forever,
Giving light and love and hope
To all who gaze
And wish
Upon
A star.

Cool Cat

The cat cools herself in the summer heat.
She stretches long and lean;
She grows before your eyes,
Her body taunt like a bow.
She is the arrow,
Ready to spring
In flight—
For fun, for food, for fear.

Her eyes are closed now,
Perfectly happy,
Perfectly content,
To be a cat.

Picture This

What makes me feel good:
Votive candles burning in my Santa Monica apartment
Singing when people are listening
A sensitive kiss
A sincere compliment
An open smile
Rehearsing a play
Meeting someone new I like
A clean bathroom
Making love with a "lover"
Buying something new
Talking with my cat
Writing this!

Feather, Fly Lightly

(St. Francis Hotel, San Francisco, 1968)

Lie still, little child;
Evening's nigh.
Listen while I sing you
This lullaby.

Let yourself float—
Float so free.
Close your eyes now,
And a feather you'll see.

Feather, fly lightly.
Go on now.
Fly so freely;
Show me how.

Where will you go?
How long will it take?
How many journeys
Will you make?

Weightless little feather,
With the wind as your aim—
I fear you'll fall soon
With the evening rain.

Make haste, little friend,
Go catch the breeze,
Or rest for a while
In the far-off trees.

Although I can't go,
Fly on by.
Go without me;
Take to the sky.

Feather, fly lightly,
Fly from my hand;
Fly so freely
To your far-off land.

Sleep, My Soul

Sleep, my soul.
The willow shades your sorrow,
Weeping in time with your tears of tomorrow—
No regret, no shame, no one to blame,
For it is only another day that passes
To help us heal, to see, to further our journey
On the wisdom trail of our spirit train.

We are but a minute, a speck, a sob;
We are forever, wherever we are.
Time will only mark a space we traveled;
It is only this moment that marks this thought.
Be gentle and kind to your sweet selves
As we slumber in life's moments,
Awaiting the day where all will awaken to Love.

Transitions

This Day

(for Barbara)

Remember this day.
It was always here —
Always waiting to be held
Like a flower.
Ah, so sweet the scent,
So clear the colors,
So good to be holding
This day.

To feel the petals fall
Like hours on the hills,
Painting memories with
Loving sounds
On the heels of
This day.

We skip and run
And hold hands
As we twirl round and
Round 'til we drop
With laughter,
Holding our bellies hard,
Catching our breath.

It's now we hold—
And held deeply—
Within the child,
Inside the love of friendship.
It waits for us.
It will always be there for us on
This day.

Shift

I've been moved today,
And I don't know how.
I've been moved today,
And I don't know when.

The space is new.
When did I arrive?
It happened today,
The most unlikely of days.

Did I move today,
Or was a mountain removed?
Or the last pebble?

I feel the void of negativity,
And I mourn for the cover.

Why these tears?
Why now?
Life is good, life is full.

Yet, the longing—
Oh, the longing so deep in my soul
It aches.
I'm in love, but there is no one there.
Is it with myself?
Ah, an answer.

Leafing

And the breeze said to the leaf:
"Sometimes you blow away the things
That don't care for you,
And sometimes the things that do
And would remain with you.

"But, alas, I am but a breeze,
With only seeing and being
Free and wild and gentle
Just as I am—
No direction do I know
Where I blow."

And as the breeze lifted the leaf with a sigh,
He kissed it goodbye,
And his cry echoed down the empty street:
"Leafing is so har-r-r-r-r-r-r-r-r-rd!"

Brink in 1990

And now we sit and wait
For no one—
But, ah, the feelings that come that
Pull up from the belly
And into the tittering mind of despair.

Despair for me,
Despair for us.

I don't know what happy is—
A temporary moment of belonging to
Something deemed important.

But, ah, when that something leaves us—
We tear ourselves apart with unbelief.

To love oneself:
That is the answer.
Oh, but to know oneself:
Therein lies the truth.

Blame

There are so many of us aching for truth.
To be blinded by what people call desires
Masks us from all the beauty within,
When we want something so bad we
Could taste it and see nothing else.

But then we enter into our own prison.
We put the bars in place and lock the door
And start to cry why no one will let us out.

Open your hand:
The key is there.

Believe

The maiden is running wild,
Flying high.
Not even a saint could catch her.
How could I?

Oh, rock of ages —
Oh, why can't I see
That all of the angels
Are really like me?

There's nothing that I feel
That you haven't, too.
So why do I feel
So distant from you?

I fear what you're seeing
Is only a face,
When the light unseen,
Untouched in its place,

Is something that lives
That forever will burn—
Love, just pure love,
In my hand I will turn.

It's the song of the children,
The song of the wind.
Believe, just believe,
Who you are to the end.

Milly

An explosion of light.
Slight perception of sound.
A crackle,
Like a faint firework exploding, then cascading.
I saw it up high in the air
In my bedroom last night—
The night
Milly died.

Milly:
The atheist
The political activist
Sierra Club hiking leader
Artist, actress, mother
Spitfire, hot lover—
Your honesty hurt to the bone.

A joyful but sad
One-way conversation
On the night
Milly died:

I told her, "Come and explode in on me anytime;
I'll take you dead or alive."
My Milly—
How you made us laugh,
My beloved friend.

Fall Down, Leaves
(Ode to Autumn)

Fall down, leaves.
Give the tree a rest.
She has carried your weight;
Now cover her breast.

She needs your protection,
So sail down to the ground.
Be her noble protector
As you gather all around.

Fall down, leaves,
Ne'er to be green again.
Your golden days are here
As you slowly descend.

Without voice you proclaim
The depth of your love,
As you lay down the life
You once had above.

So fall down, leaves.
The tree bows as you do—
To your supreme sacrifice,
In humble gratitude.

She has given you life.
You have given her shade.
And we are blessed to see
How love is truly made.

October Past

'Twas every day a good time for laughter.
Peals like bells on hilltops rang
O'er the town's houses, children running.

Gaily we played in breathless wonder,
Becoming whatever whim delivered its message,
Taking apart the masks of humanity one by one.

Carelessly abandoning the characters we knew,
Wildly shrieking with no understanding
As we mocked our way through the day.

Hitting upon deeply held truths,
We bounced them about—
Randomly, unknowingly, tossing them aside.

For what do they matter, these great
Unspoken truths innocently uttered
Without the joy that fills the child's heart?

Oh, to see life as a butterfly of delight
And sorrow, something to giggle at
Behind the azalea bushes.

The Lady from the Sky
(for Claudia)

The dry part of our hearts
We showered with deep discussions
About God and life.
The ground started to bud,
Becoming full of life,
And you walked into your garden
And without hesitation
You chose your rose,
Plucked it up tenderly,
And walked away.

Fly now, my beautiful winged friend.
I helped you feel safe on the ground,
And it was good.
But your grandeur is in
The sky where you live,
Giving hope to those who want
To try,
To fly,
Like the lady from the sky.

Forgives You

You hurt me—
White blazing pain—
The black part of you
Like a cloak
Covering, stifling, my girl self,
As you laughed,
Robbing me of my inklings
And beginnings of self-love.
You took these from me,
And you laughed
While I cried, choking,
With sand in my mouth.

You, you father—
Your hatred settled between my eyes,
Where you took your aim.
How I hated myself for being so hated by you.
How tortured my soul—
The ripping of my natural, good kind eyes,
Blinding me of my beauty
As you laughed.

Then I awakened.
And I saw it was you,
You all along,
Not me, who was the sick one.
It was you—
The one who was soul sick,
Hating his daughter.
You were soul sick
To want me less,
To want me broken.
And I searched
And searched
And found my Self,
And found the strength
To pick up my bed and walk,
Walk away from your Satan face
And Satan eyes of lies and mockery.
I walked away
Out the door,
And oh, oh, I hated you more.

I hated you for my self-hatred.
I hated you for hating me.
And there was hate,
Pure hate—
Hurtful, disintegrating, mutilating hate.
It tore at me,
Eating my peace,
Tearing my heart.

But then
The day came,
And I knew
I hurt only me,
Only me,
Only me—
I hurt only me to hate back.

But I had to hate you
Fierce and so hard.
It shook me with the knowledge of who you really are—
A broken, sick, shattered self of a man who could
Despise his precious little girl.
Yes, broken—
You are the broken one,
Who could not break his daughter.

And I stand now at your grave.
I look down at you —
Me above,
You below —
And I lift my eyes and reach up to my Heavenly Father,
Who loves me.

And I know I am loved.
And I have self-worth.
And I have self-love.
And I know I am good,
And I am whole.

And I know what I must do:
The voice whispered to me,
Softly, clear, and true.

And I can now,
And I need to,
And I want to,
And I do:
For me, not for you,
Completely and totally,
All of me . . .
Forgives you.

Mother

The master puppeteer is sick,
No strings on her fingers,
No playing her children,
Her husband.
We are fallen marionettes.
What will we do?

Women

Women.
We feel it all.
We are the nerve center
Of the universe.

It is our lot to bear,
So we do it,
And we lead the way for other women
As other women have done before us,
Proudly,
Sometimes quietly,
Sometimes loudly,
Gracefully,
Sometimes not,
But always with dignity.

Vietnam

(in loving memory of our boys who died in Vietnam)

So sad.
They will never see their
Children's eyes—
The boys
Who could have been men,
Who became soldiers instead.
They died

Forever
On foreign soil,
Their young hands no longer
Entwined in their lovers' hands.
Now
One with the forgiven enemy,
Part of the land they never knew.

Before now,
Before their voices dropped,
Before hair grew on their chest:
 Vietnam,
 A place on the globe,
 Not to die.

Vietnam,
We carry your babies
Of regret and sorrow.
Our blood runs
Through your mines
And veins:
 Vietnam,
 You were just a name.

Time

This thing called Time has a life all its own.
Forget about it, and it stands still.
Embrace it, and it's on your side.
Resist it, and it feels forever.
Love it, and it flies by.

Time, where do you go?
Do you get old too?
Or do you just stop when we do?
What funny tricks you play;
You must laugh a lot.
I think I like you, Time, that way.

Hunger Pangs

There's a stirring in my soul
I haven't felt in so long a time—
A quivering of new thoughts,
A restless longing for new,
A breaking-out feeling of the edges,
Of the should-bes,
A redefining of the lines drawn
Of what's right for me.
We can erase any form drawn
And start anew again.
How about this one?
Be your own best friend!

Just One Year

(for Larry)

Stirs my soul,
Touching the sadness;
Not old memories
But new tears:
Just one year,
Just one year—
The anniversary of your dying.

God, it makes me wonder.
God, it makes me cry.
God, it makes me want to know more.

Another Christmas

Another Christmas,
Another lonely holy day,
Another time to lay down,
The awful words of hurt.

Smile, even if untrue;
Nod in agreement if you don't.
For it's another Christmas;
We cannot disappoint.

The happiest time of year—
Can we just be near
The star that shone in
The East to lead the wise men
To the One,
The baby Jesus?

Put aside hatred and
Resentments,
And put on
The pajamas of love.

Wind in Winter

It starts with a whisper
At the far corners of the mouth of life.
Quietly it comes around the bend,
Swirling in the moments of a quick glance,
Wrapping around the skirts of innocence,
Gushing down and over mountains of delight,
Laughing as it shakes the leaves to the ground,
Tossing them like a huge nature salad
Up and then down and up again,
Not knowing where they scatter
Or whose eyes see the child snuggled
Inside the fur of a sleepy puppy,
Whose day was spent in outrageous splendor,
Wrestling and running as one with the
Wind in winter.

The Girl and the Rock

Act I

There was a little girl who was lost in the desert. She didn't know where to go to get water. As she lay on the desert sand, she saw in the distance what looked to be an ancient well. Weary and all alone, the girl allowed her gaze to fall on another object that was closer by. It was a very large rock.

The little girl had a decision to make. She felt intimidated by the well's appearance and by how far away it seemed. And although she had seen a well before, she had never used one. She was quite suspicious and mistrustful of what she might find at the bottom of its deep, dark hole. So she chose instead to go to the more familiar and closer rock.

Act II

Inch by painful inch, the little girl willed her aching body forward until she found herself so close to the rock that her parched lips brushed up against its shiny blackness.

"Please, Rock, I am dying of thirst. Could you spare a small drink of water?"

The rock appeared strong, safe, and noble. The little girl was sure it had lived there forever in the sand, and so she thought it must be very wise and possess a reliable source of water.

But the rock replied, "I cannot give you water."

This caught the little girl by surprise. The rock must

not have understood her. Surely the rock would comply once she made herself clearer. "Oh please, Rock," she said a little louder. "I shall perish if you do not give me some of your water."

Again the rock replied, "I am a rock. I cannot give you water."

The little girl began to sob and wail. In an act of desperation, she threw her frail little body over the rock, pleading. But the rock said nothing.

Wiping the tears from her face, the little girl began to think. She remembered the bright colored crayons she kept hidden in the deep pockets of her dress, and she dug them out. With new resolution, she found the strength to draw.

"Ah ha!" she thought. "I will change the rock into someone nice — someone I can talk to." And she drew friendly little faces all over the rock, with beautiful smiles, and for a while she was happy. "Dear Rock, dear friend. You look so sweet and alive. Would you please give me water now?"

"I am a rock. I cannot give you water," the rock said with the same steady voice.

The rock's reply made the little girl furious, and her fury gave her a new sense of power. She grabbed the rock and tried with all her might to lift it from the desert floor, but the rock was much too big for her little hands. Indeed, even if her hands had been ten times bigger and she had been ten times stronger, she still wouldn't have budged it.

Finally, in total exhaustion, the little girl collapsed on the rock. She prayed that a drop of water would somehow fall onto her dry, cracked lips. She remained lying there for two days and two nights. She felt certain that the rock approved of her suffering and so would change its mind, as she bore the freezing cold of night and withstood the blazing desert sun of day. But the rock shared not a drop of water.

Act III

At last, on the third morning, the little girl dragged herself up from the rock and onto her swollen feet. She was dirty, her spirit was broken, and she knew she was dying. She began to speak, but then hesitated and decided to keep silent. Staring at the rock for a very long time, she slowly and regretfully turned away.

The little girl managed to stay on her shaky little legs as she limped her way over to the ancient well some distance away. Teetering side to side, she steadied herself on the wall of the well as she searched for the handle. When she found it, she began to turn it, round and round. She watched warily as the old wooden bucket slowly descended into the dark, scary hole.

The little girl thought she heard a faint splashing sound as she leaned slightly over the opening of the well. The sound caused her heart to jump and adrenaline to shoot through her body. Instinctively, she began to turn the handle in reverse. Something wonderful was happening. The bucket was rising up out of the well.

The little girl was filled with wonder, and tears of gratitude ran down her face to see the bucket filled with pure, precious, cool water. She drank and drank and drank.

Epilogue

With her thirst quenched and the strength restored to her body, the little girl walked back to the rock proudly. With a straightened back and a new sense of calm in her voice, she said, "I understand now. You are a rock, and you cannot give water."

The rock was silent and did not move—for it was a rock.

Sigh

Sigh deeply,
And remember:
These are the days of
Remembrance—
Each moment
Ne'er to pass again.

Prayer Food

May This Be Yours

May there come a time in your life
When all the sorrow you have had is likened
To a drop of water in the ocean
Compared to one ounce of pure love
That you have been blessed to drink.

Only love—
That's all that matters,
That is real,
That is lasting,
That is love.

Be Still

Be still, frightened heart.
I will be here to comfort you in the night.
I am faith,
I am hope,
I am love.
I hold you in my embrace
To lighten your fears;
Give them to me.
Trust in the goodness
Of your beautiful soul.

Eternal Love

The simple truth has always been
The candle that burns within—
The glow we feel when all is well—
Is always there, is burning still.
When faith is waning and heads are low,
The eternal One will heal you
Because God told us so.

Going Beyond

Tormented souls only see through bars.
The light falls in stripes on their swollen faces.
Trapped men—
Twisted hands wrought with worry,
Mouths open in silent screams.
The dreams
Seen written on forgotten foreheads,
Huddled in corners;
Closer, it feels better to touch.
Why must it hurt so much?

Oh God, don't let me die uninspired
In my jail of unfulfilled desires.
I will reach out to the crack in the wall,
Where light is gently calling.
I see nothing else
As I get up and walk
To the opening of my soul.

One

Passion
Is life
Is all of it
Encircling life
Death
Mourning
Celebration
The end
The beginning
Omega

It is the sound of
The earth
The animals
Breaking hearts
Children
Fire
Laughter
Beauty
Changing
Evolving
Moving

Is one universe
One world
One people
One cry
One voice
One sound
Of passion

The Truth

Hearken, oh my friend,
Lost soul now found—
You are awakening.
The light is bright;
It soothes your troubled heart.

Be not discouraged.
Your way has always been lit;
You were just standing in
The shadows of doubt.

Friend

How blessed to have a friend who will tell you:
"Open your eyes. It's right there, see?"

And sure enough,
The light from your friend's eyes and heart
Is cast upon the ground,
And like magic
The world is right again.

The Decision

The power is within me to change—
To change all things that I never thought I could.
Today I can be who I want to be;
This moment I will be living my dream.

Thoughts are what my life reflects back to me;
The mystery is locked in this.
I want to change the reflections,
Replace the mirrors, the old broken glass.

The Cloud Lifts

A teacher must learn
Before he can teach.
He must do and see and feel,
And then know,
Before he can help you to know,
Or do, see, and feel.

Why does it hurt to write?
It should feel good to
Purge myself of anxieties
With new thought forms
That are suddenly revealed
On paper.

I don't want
Confusion, pain, or
Impatience.
God, help me help myself
Before I can help others.
The flow should be simple, pure, and fun.
Life, be gentle—
I am your struggling servant;
I open my arms to your
Sweetness
And to the soft steady rain
Of oneness.

A New World

Many faces turn toward the East—
Enlightenment, new life,
And mysteries untold.
Behold:
We are at the threshold of peace;
It is foretold.

A great birth is taking place, but first
Waves and waves of death and despair.
But the darkness will end,
And suffering shall cease.

This is a given—
What we humans are headed toward,
Thrashing and flailing as we go.
Temples of light await us, with
Love unimaginable.
Have faith;
It is coming to pass:
A new world.

God of Sound

Oh, dear God of sound,
You speak and we are made
In your image.

Middle-aged in Pasadena,
A troubadour still—
Love escapes me;
Maybe it always will.

Ah, but hope burns bright.
The morrow I long to see;
My dreams they peek
Their heads out to greet me.

Onward

I leave behind the clothes I wore yesterday.
Colors now abound in bright splashes
Of light all around me—
My new clothes of light,
Crystal, and laughter:
I wear love;
I wear joy.
See how it drapes around me.
I dance to celebrate my being.
I honor my healing.
I give thanks to my Lord.

I Have Been

This has been a long road—
The one I didn't know I was on.
I thought fate had tossed me up
To throw me down,
But now I know it was me all along.

    I have been the captain,
    I have been the slave,
    I have been the tormentor,
    And I was the love never made.

It was me all along—
All along this road,
How far to go was a red light of my own.
Like diners with booths lined in suede,
I bought the tickets to the movies I made.

    I have been the cheater,
    I have been the con,
    I have been the leaver,
    And the heartache in sad songs.

All the time my heart held the answer
To the cry for love I sent to the sky.
Always "out there," I cursed and pleaded
To the shut doors, the tears and goodbyes.

I have been the white knight,
I have been the friend,
I have been the magic,
And I will be forever
And ever—
Amen.

Home

I no longer want to live in this world of illusions
Where everything is just a mirror of the real thing—
A maze full of wrong turns, pitfalls, and imaginings.

I long for a world where eyes meet and know
That the look is a simple exchange of love,
Not meant to implore, manipulate, or deceive.

Oh, give me a place where true hearts give;
That is where I want to live—
Where there is nothing to forgive.

Prayer Food

I pray for serenity—
    To hear God's answers as he speaks to me
    Through others, through silence, through all things
        Seen and unseen.

I pray for courage—
    To weather the storms as they blow through my door,
    Causing upheaval and unbalancing the steadiest of
        souls.

I pray for others—
    That they may feel and know how essential they are
    To everyone, to feel important being human with great
        faith in life.

I pray for myself—
    That I may continue my search for peace by
        discovering
    New ways and disciplines to heal myself and applying
        them daily.

Hallelujah

One day
We will walk on paths with no rocks,
When light will brighten the way.
We will hear the music of the angels
And will see the mountains of time
Rise above us in silhouettes of love—
Deep, darkened clouds of faith above,
Ready to spill down on humankind.

All questions answered,
All cries soothed,
And each baby born
With heavenly laughter
Will sing hallelujah,
Hallelujah,
One day.

I Will Sing You Home

So dream on,
My white eagle bird.
Sail on high with the angels,
And I will sing you home.

LYRICS

Hometown Beauty Queen

I was told long ago,
When movies were picture shows,
There was only one thing to be:
The hometown beauty queen.

I did what I was told,
Twirled around in my crown of gold.
All the Shriners smiled at me,
Their hometown beauty queen.

Turn it on for the judges—
Another quarter turn, please.
Ten points for her charm,
But she's a little knock-kneed.
Well, she's no Rita Hayworth,
But she's as good as we can make
For our local hopeful in the year of '68.

So I took my diet pills
To make my waistline thinner still,
Learned to walk up and down stairs
With three books on top of my hair.

Did you know that Vaseline
Is an old trick of beauty queens?
You smear it all over your teeth—
You smile great but you can't speak.

Turn it on for the judges—
Another quarter turn, please.
Ten points for her charm,
But she's a little knock-kneed.
Well, she's no Rita Hayworth.
But she's as good as we can make
For our local hopeful in the year of '68

I was in fighting shape,
Living just on protein shakes,
With an Ex-Lax or two for lunch—
Now a girl can't lose too much.

Bathing suits and high-heel shoes,
Wondering who would win or lose,
Coming together to meet the best,
Scared of who was prettiest.

I was in the chosen ten—
Frozen smile and suckin' in.
My hometown's eyes on me,
Watching on their local TV.
Then we took our final spin,
Only five girls left to win.
The women libbers marched and cried,
While the men sat and judged our thighs.

Turn it on for the cameras, turn it on for Mom and Dad—
And for the little girl waiting to get the winner's
    autograph.
Well, the title you didn't take, Miss America you'll never
    make,
But you'll always be the hometown beauty queen of '68.

I was told long ago,
When movies were picture shows,
There was only one thing to be:
My mother's fantasy—
Go on now,
Be a good girl, win for me.

A Sad Victory

I was driving down the street today
When I saw him standing there,
More gray in his hair—
I guess you might say
He looked worse for the wear.

I stopped to say hello.
I thought that it would be good
And my pity not be misunderstood.
Then I remembered how he made me cry
And why.

The reasons don't matter anymore,
No point to try and even up the score.
Life has a way of doing that just fine,
When all your time is making money,
And all your love is drinking wine.

He was smoking a cigarette
In his ol' familiar way—
Like it was yesterday.
He was so sure back then—
Where was his cocky grin?

All I saw were his shaking hands,
While he was talking of used-to-bes.
I pretended not to see,
But when push came to shove
He was only in love with a picture of me.

His eyes were sad and unsure,
And when the moment came to part,
Would I have a change of heart?
But I didn't cave in to the money and wine
And what might have been.

It was a final farewell to the past
And to those I thought were friends—
To the ghosts that looked like him.
This was a meant-to-be
But, all in all, a sad victory.

And the reasons don't matter anymore,
No point to try and even up the score.
Life has a way of doing that just fine,
When all your time is making money,
And all your love is drinking wine.

Sailor Man

He came in from the sea
Or was it Kentucky?
With dimples for miles and miles,
A little drunk and always wild—
A swaggart when he walked,
Ah, but a poet when he talked.
He's just a lonely man,
Makes me wonder who I am.

And just when I think he's gone,
An ocean breeze will come along,
And his laugh will fill the air
As if he couldn't have a care,
And he stands and looks at me
With flashing eyes that always see.
Yes, he knows I love the man,
Makes me wonder who I am.

In his heart and mind and soul,
He's a sailor from long ago,
Never to be caught and tied.
Godspeed, my love,
For you I would die.

When I need your company,
You're out dancing with the sea,
The seaweed flying as you twirl
In your dark and stormy world.
So have your maiden fair—
You love me best when I'm not there.
My lover dear, my sailor man,
You make me wonder who I am.

Let's turn the hands of time
Back to when you were all mine.
The ale was good and life was bad,
And you and I were all we had.
But, oh, we were happy then,
And I remember when
You cried and kissed my hand
And said, "I have to go, please understand."

"In my heart and mind and soul,
I'm a sailor from long ago,
Never to be caught and tied.
Godspeed, my love, for you I would die"

And you come back now and then
To make sure you have your friend.
Yes, I'll be there till I die,
Or until the oceans all run dry,
And then I'll have you all for me—
No sad goodbyes, no lover's grief.
No, no, you love her best,
And my soul she will never rest.

In your heart and mind and soul,
You're a sailor from long ago,
Never to be caught and tied.
Godspeed, my love, for you I would die.

The sea, my immortal enemy
And you, my windblown destiny

In his heart and mind and soul,
He's a sailor from long ago,
Never to be caught and tied.
Godspeed, my love, for you I would die.

The American Family

He was a man of simple means,
A blue collar worker in old blue jeans.
He lived in Los Angeles with three little girls and Annie.

He was a printer in a big company,
Got lost in the shuffle of bureaucracy.
He worked real hard and never complained,
And every night he came home to Annie.

Oh, Annie packed his lunch every day,
And Steve would faithfully bring home his pay.
The little girls would want new things—
Petticoats, bicycles, and ice cream.

Oh, the married woman and man,
You know they're doing the best they can
To put food on their table and give love and security—
Oh, the American family.

He got a gold watch from the company,
And Steve gave them twenty-seven years' working
    honestly.
Now their dog is getting fat.
The girls are gone and grown; they're all alone.

Annie says, "Steve, you know, you eat too much."
Then they argue about what they're gonna have for
    lunch.
Then he goes out for a walk,
And Annie calls the girls to have a talk.

She says, "I hope I go before your daddy does—
I don't know what I'd do without that ornery cuss."
Then he walks back through the door,
And there they go again, pickin' on each other some more.

Oh, the married woman and man,
You know they're doing the best they can
To put food on their table and give love and security—
Oh, the American family.

Oh say, can you see?

Maybe I'll Go There

I wish I was in Houston—
Oh, I wish I could be there,
Where nobody knows me
And nobody cares.
In Houston—
Maybe I'll go there.

I wish I was in Miami—
Oh, I wish I could be there,
Catch a fish in the ocean
On a real bright day.
In Miami—
That's where I'll stay.

> Oh, my baby don't love me anymore;
> He said he don't need me like before,
> And when I cried
> He closed the door.

I wish I was in Mexico—
Where Latin men would love to kiss my hand;
We'll take a siesta
In the afternoon.
In Mexico—
I'll be there soon. . . .

Maybe . . . I'll go there.

Man of My Dreams

Last night I dreamed a beautiful dream—
A vision of you,
The colors so true.

Your hand held a ring;
You told me something,
But I couldn't hear.
I couldn't hear.

> Man of my dreams,
> Who could you be?
> What did you say?
> Why do I feel this way?
> How could I know
> That I could love you so?
> And that you will always be
> The man of my dreams.

There's a place I can go,
Where only dream lovers know,
Where nobody leaves
And nobody changes.

Tonight I'll dream my beautiful dream,
And never awake to this world again,
If that's all it takes
To make you come true.
Then I'll close my eyes
And fly to you.

Man of my dreams,
Who could you be?
What did you say?
Why do I feel this way?
How could I know
That I could love you so?
And that you will always be
The man of my dreams.

God's Sweet Lullaby

Raindrops falling on a roof,
Little cats purring loud,
Crickets chirping at the moon,
And leaves falling down.

Soft winds blowing through the trees
Are the loveliest sighs;
Close your eyes and hear the songs
Of angels in disguise.

And you can hear it if you try—
And you can hear it, God's sweet lullaby.
Rock you gently, fast asleep.
Soothe your soul for to keep,
When you hear God's sweet lullaby.

Fishes jumping in a pond
To the frog's croaking sound,
Night bird singing, "Day is done,"
Till morning comes round.

All these voices in the night
Are whispering low
That the world is full of love.
They're letting us know

That we can hear it if we try—
We can hear it, God's sweet lullaby.
Rock you gently, fast asleep.
Soothe your soul for to keep,
When you hear God's sweet lullaby—
When we can hear God's sweet lullaby.

About the Poet

Jo Anne Kurman is a twenty-first–century troubadour, having been a professional singer and guitarist since she was sixteen years old. Her first music job was at Disneyland, playing one of their famous Hootenanny Nights with a folk group called The Fourmost. That same night they shared the bill with a skinny young singer named Hoyt Axton.

Jo Anne's musical adventures range from playing in a bluegrass band in Montie Montana Jr.'s Buffalo Bill's Wild West Show in Jakarta, Indonesia, to singing backup for Iron Butterfly in the "20 Years After: Woodstock Reunion Concert." She won Nashville's *Music Row Magazine*'s Discovery Award for her CD *Hometown Beauty Queen*; performed as the opening act for Billy Preston, Sawyer Brown, and Lee Greenwood; and has sung on many radio and television commercials. In 2008, Jo Anne was honored to perform for former First Lady Nancy Reagan at a Fourth of July celebration, as well as kicking off her career as a record producer with Al Timss's jazz CD *Last Call*.

Jo Anne's inspiration for writing her song "Hometown Beauty Queen" came from the combined experience of winning and surviving the titles of Miss Inglewood, Miss Los Angeles County, and Second Runner-up to Miss California the year she turned eighteen. In her senior year of college, she cofounded the Burbage Theater in Hermosa Beach, California, where she acted in and musical-directed a number of plays and musicals. Jo Anne was honored with a Drama-Logue Award for Most Outstanding Performance as the lead in *Death of a Miner* and graduated cum laude from California State University, Long Beach with a BA in Theater Arts.

As a songwriter, Jo Anne coauthored songs with Randall Pugh and Ron Guffnett that charted in the top ten of the

Top 100 Country Hits across Europe. She has cowritten songs with Sandy Sherman that have been used in many television movies. A recent booking was at the beautiful Montage Hotel in Laguna Beach, California, where she performed a single act. The year 2009 proved to be a landmark for Jo Anne. Besides her poetry book, *Dreams for Sale*, and the completion of *Countrified*, a new CD, she landed her first national television commercial as an actress.

Jo Anne's secret to what keeps her reaching for the stars is her unshakable belief that the best is yet to come. In fact, if you ever happen to be in her kitchen, take a look at her refrigerator door. You'll find words posted of her favorite saying, by Winston Churchill: "Never, never, never give up!"

You can reach Jo Anne through her website: joannekurman.com.

About the Artist

Based in Los Angeles with his lovely wife and two exceptionally bright and beautiful children, Chris Davies has been creating his unique vision of art for over thirty years. He began his art career as a freelance illustrator after graduating with honors from Art Center College of Design, Pasadena, California, in 1990. To see more of Chris's art, visit his blog at cdaviesart.blogspot.com.

Jo Anne Kurman's CDs

Jo Anne has the following CDs available:

Hometown Beauty Queen

Jo Anne's debut album consists of eleven original compositions. The style of music is a cross-section of folk, pop, and country. Lyrics for three of the eleven songs recorded are included in her poetry book *Dreams for Sale*. They are:

"Hometown Beauty Queen"
"The American Family"
"Maybe I'll Go There"

500 Miles

This CD is Jo Anne's tribute to folk music, and consists of the following classic folk songs from the 1960s and 1970s:

"Diamonds and Rust"
"500 Miles"
"Me and Bobby McGee"
"Muddy Old River"
"Annie's Song"
"Someday Soon"
"Suzanne"
"The Night They Drove Old Dixie Down"
"Both Sides, Now"
"Snowbird"
"Four Strong Winds"
"Mr. Tambourine Man"

Countrified

This CD is a collection of Jo Anne's favorite original country songs, which she either wrote herself or cowrote with some special songwriting friends.

Ordering Jo Anne's CDs and Books

For information on ordering her CDs and books, contact Jo Anne at joannekurman.com. You can also order Jo Anne's books at amazon.com. For wholesale book orders, contact BookSurge at 866-308-6235.

COLOPHON

The text and titling are set in Meridien, created in the mid-1950s by the Swiss designer Adrian Frutiger (who also designed Univers, which, in tandem with Helvetica, convincingly demonstrated that sans serif typefaces could be used in body text without sacrificing readability). The section and part titling is in Skia, produced in the early 1990s by the designer of Galliard, Matthew Carter. Both designers are currently active. —D.B.

Made in the USA